Cyber bullying

by Heather E. Schwartz

Consultant:
Frank W. Baker
Media Literacy Consultant
Media Literacy Clearinghouse Inc.

CAPSTONE PRESS
a capstone imprint

Fact Finders are published by Capstone Press,
1710 Roe Crest Drive, North Mankato, Minnesota 56003
www.capstonepub.com

Library of Congress Cataloging-in-Publication Data
Schwartz, Heather E.
 Cyberbullying / by Heather E. Schwartz.
   p. cm.—(Fact finders. tech safety smarts.)
 Includes bibliographical references and index.
 Summary: "Describes cyberbullying and ways to prevent or stop cyberbullying
attacks"—Provided by publisher.
 ISBN 978-1-4296-9944-0 (library binding) — ISBN 978-1-62065-798-0 (pbk.)
 ISBN 978-1-4765-1573-1 (eBook PDF)
 1. Cyberbullying—Juvenile literature. 2. Internet and children—Juvenile literature.
I. Title.
 HV6773.15.C92S39 2013
 302.34'302854678—dc23   2012020253

Editorial Credits
Jennifer Besel, editor; Sarah Bennett, designer; Laura Manthe, production specialist

Photo Credits
Dreamstime: Cammeraydave, 14; iStockphotos: Christa Brunt, 16, CountryStyle
Photography, 20; Shutterstock: Aleksandr Bryliaev, 22 (like icons), Apollofoto, 28
(person), beboy, 7 (phone), BORTEL Pavel, 17 (inset), Cheryl Casey, 10 (person),
ColinCramm, 4 (inset), ETIENjones, 21, Farsh, 17 (jail), iconspro, 7 (speech
icon), Irina_QQQ, 12, 14-15 (background), James Thew, 11, javi merino, 28, 29
(avatars), karen roach, 25, kostudio, 9 (person), Kraska, 4 (phone), Maria Egupova,
10, 24 (avatar), Maridav, 24 (middle), Mathias Rosenthal, 26, mhatzapa, 26-27
(background), Michael D Brown, 6, MilaLiu, 7 (email icon), Nataliia Natykach,
19 (traffic lights), nmedia, 18, ostill, 12 (person), Paula kc, 27, s_buckley, 13,
stockyimages, 24 (bottom), Timea, 9 (diagram), VLADGRIN, cover (icons)

Artistic Effects
Shutterstock: antishock, Bennyart, berkut, file404, Irina_QQQ, John T Takai, Mikhail,
nrt, SoooInce, VLADGRIN

Printed in the United States of America in Stevens Point, Wisconsin.
082013   007683R

Table of Contents

What Is Cyberbullying?

Imagine giving up your cell phone and computer. No more texting your friends. No more posting online. No way!

But what if a bully started **stalking** you online? How would you feel about technology then? Cyberbullies are people who go online to spoil your fun. They spread mean messages, **rumors**, and threats. Even if cyberbullying has never happened to you, you've probably heard of it. Maybe you've even seen it.

What a loser!
8:17pm Today
From: 555-753-0824

stalk—to track a person in a secret way

rumor—something said by many people although it may not be true

Whatever your experience, cyberbullies shouldn't keep you offline. **Cyberbullies don't deserve that kind of power.** Make sure they don't get control by protecting yourself from their attacks.

Knowing they're out there is your first defense. Understanding how and why cyberbullies do what they do can also help. And if you're attacked, there are steps to take to make sure bullies don't get the best of you. Keep reading to see how you can keep your online life useful, safe, and fun.

Talk about It

Throughout this book, you'll find "Talk about It" boxes that set up real-life situations you might run into. Use these boxes as discussion starters at home or at school. Talk about the pros and cons of different actions, and decide how you could stay safe in each situation.

So suppose you get a text from an unknown number. The text says to watch your back tomorrow at school.

What do you do?

Being Cyberbullied

The target of a cyberbully usually can't miss the signs. Victims receive nasty messages by text or e-mail. They read rumors about themselves on social networking sites. They might spot embarrassing photos of themselves all over the Internet. Some cyberbullies even set up websites about their victims, asking others to post comments.

Have you ever read a mean comment about yourself online or received a harsh text? If so, you're not alone. A 2011 survey by Yoursphere.com found more than one in three kids has been cyberbullied.

A Word about Drama

A lot of kids don't call online problems "cyberbullying." They might describe it as "drama" instead. Cyberbullies are often called "haters." It doesn't matter what you call it. People using technology to scare or embarrass others is never OK.

Is It Cyberbullying?

You and a friend have an argument at school. That evening your friend sends text messages threatening to beat you up the next time she sees you.

Is it cyberbullying?

Yes.

Even friends can become cyberbullies if they threaten you with physical harm.

A classmate disagrees with your opinion on a message board. In fact, he disagrees so strongly that he uses all caps to "shout" in his post.

Is it cyberbullying?

No.

It's OK to voice different opinions. Just be sure no one is attacked personally.

Someone—you're not sure who—**hacks** into your computer. He or she sends out nasty e-mails to your friends from your account.

Is it cyberbullying?

Yes.

When someone is trying to make you look like a cyberbully, you're actually the target. The cyberbully is trying to hurt you by turning your friends against you.

hack—to break into a computer system illegally

Are You the Cyberbully?

Have you ever posted something you thought was funny, but then later you found out your statement upset someone? Or have you read a rumor in an e-mail and just had to pass it on to your friends? In these situations your actions hurt someone else. You've become a cyberbully—even if you didn't mean to.

Most cyberbullying isn't accidental though. Starting rumors to get **revenge** or posting pictures to embarrass someone might make you feel good for the moment. But no matter what your reasons for doing it, cyberbullying is never the answer. It only makes technology unsafe for everyone.

revenge—action taken in return for an injury or offense

forwarded a funny, but not very nice, e-mail about someone?

forwarded an embarrassing photo of someone without his or her permission?

sent messages or posted commen[ts] while posing a[s] someone else?

used technology to send anonymous threats to someone you didn't like?

You've been a cyberbully. Don't be too hard on yourself though. Just make sure you don't go there again.

spread mean rumors you read online about a classmate?

tried to get someone in trouble by giving out his or her private information, such as a password or e-mail address?

pose—to pretend to be someone else

anonymous—written, done, or given by a person whose name is not known or made public

How Cyberbullying Works

There are tons of positive ways to use technology. You can keep in touch with friends. You can research new interests and hobbies. You can watch videos and play games.

But unfortunately, technology also gives bullies an edge. It's much easier to behave badly when you never come face-to-face with your victims. Plus, in cyberspace cyberbullies can easily hide who they really are.

We Hate Jenny Club
Today at 8:23pm

Jenny is so stuck up! Click "like" and join the We Hate Jenny Club.

Like - Comment 👍 11 💬 6

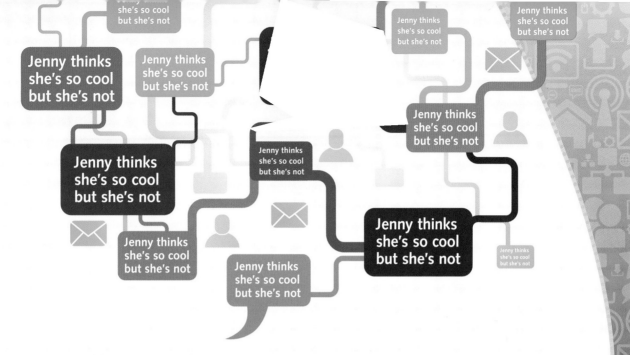

Bullies don't always do all the work. Often bullies ask friends to forward e-mail rumors or post mean comments on a social networking site. They might also share a victim's personal information with specific people or hate groups. These groups then bully the person too. This type of bullying lets one single bully hide behind a whole crowd of people.

But why would anyone want to be so mean?

TALK about it

Your best friend keeps forwarding you e-mail rumors about a classmate. You don't like getting them, and you definitely don't forward them.

But is there more you can do to stop your friend's cyberbullying behavior?

Why Do They Do It?

There are plenty of reasons why people cyberbully. It often starts out when someone believes it's deserved. What if you were getting picked on at school? You might not be able to do much about it at the moment. But at home cyberbullying might seem like a way to get revenge.

Revenge isn't the only reason for cyberbullying. Sometimes cyberbullies are just bored and looking for something to do. Sometimes they want to stir up reactions from others. These bullies don't have to see their victims react. So they can pretend what they've done doesn't matter. But each mean message or nasty post can hurt someone, whether the cyberbully knows it or not.

in the news

It might boost your confidence to know some cyberbullies are just jealous. Actress and singer Selena Gomez has spoken out about being bullied. How does she deal with cyberbullying? She tries to ignore it. "Although I can read a thousand wonderful comments, one bad comment will throw me," she said. "If I'm honest, I can be too sensitive sometimes, but I try not to focus on it."

The Effects of Cyberbullying

Cyberbullies don't always know how their attacks make victims feel. But their actions always have **consequences**. Victims of cyberbullying often experience emotional problems. They may feel scared, depressed, or anxious. Those emotional problems can lead to more trouble for victims. They might stop studying and lose interest in activities they once enjoyed. They might pull away from their friends. Often, victims can't just ignore it and go on with life as usual.

consequence—the result of an action

The consequences of cyberbullying can turn physical too. Some victims get so upset they can't sleep. They start eating more or less than they did before the bullying began. In some rare cases, victims of cyberbullying have committed **suicide**. It doesn't happen often. But this extreme action shows how much words can hurt. What you say online counts just as much as what you say offline.

In the News

Erica Gross of New York was in high school when the bullying started. A group of former friends started bullying her at school and by computer. They drew pictures of her and posted them on social networking sites. They threatened to beat her up. When stress caused her to lose weight, they used instant messaging to make mean comments.

"I had to go to my pediatrician for a physical for school, and I was labeled anorexic. I was also diagnosed with depression and anxiety," she says. "Now I live with post-traumatic stress disorder. To this day I fear seeing those girls. I never want to look at them in the face again!"

suicide—the taking of one's own life

Bullies Getting in Trouble

Consequences aren't just for victims. When cyberbullies are caught, they face consequences too. Parents often punish kids for cyberbullying by taking away cell phones, computer access, and other privileges. Internet Service Providers (ISPs) will close a person's account for cyberbullying. New laws require that schools also have rules against cyberbullying. Bullies can be suspended or even expelled from school.

In extreme cases, cyberbullying is a crime. Federal laws ban hate crimes, such as threats against a person based on his or her race. Local laws are also being passed to ban cyberbullying. If a cyberbully is caught breaking any laws, he or she could be forced to pay heavy fines or even serve jail time.

Talk about it

Your friend snaps an embarrassing photo of a classmate in the locker room. He texts the photo to you and tells you to pass it on.

What do you do?

A Safe Space

Keeping technology safe starts with knowing what's appropriate behavior online—and what's not. To decide what's OK, ask yourself how you'd act in real life. Would you make that same mean comment if you had to say it face-to-face? If the thought makes you uncomfortable, reconsider what you're writing. Also think about how your parents or guardians would react to the message. Would you want them to see it? If not, that's a red flag.

In the end, the rules of behavior online aren't so different from the rules of behavior offline. No matter who you're talking to online, treat them with respect and be kind.

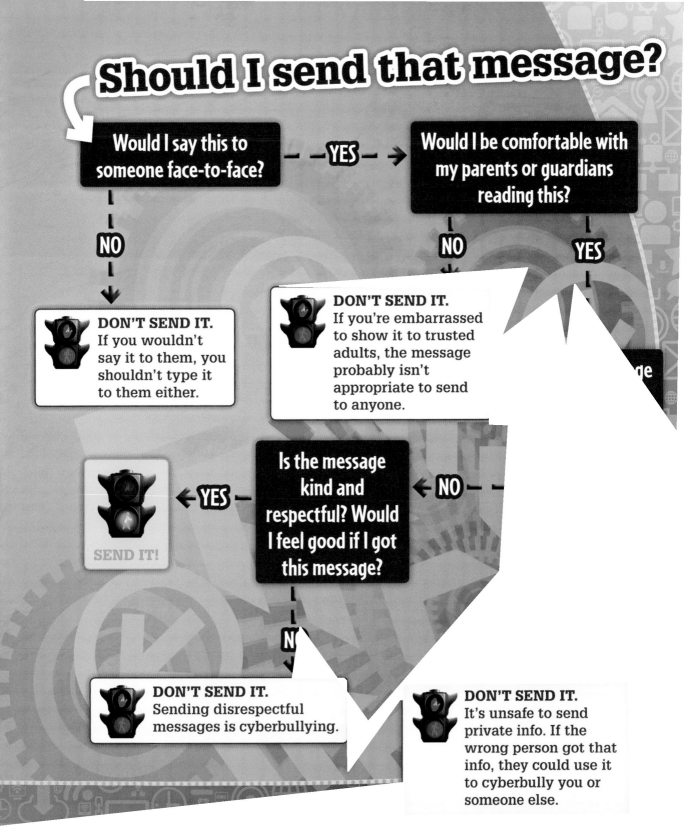

Should I send that message?

Would I say this to someone face-to-face?

— YES → **Would I be comfortable with my parents or guardians reading this?**

NO ↓

YES

NO ↓

DON'T SEND IT.
If you wouldn't say it to them, you shouldn't type it to them either.

DON'T SEND IT.
If you're embarrassed to show it to trusted adults, the message probably isn't appropriate to send to anyone.

← YES — **Is the message kind and respectful? Would I feel good if I got this message?** ← NO —

SEND IT!

NO ↓

DON'T SEND IT.
Sending disrespectful messages is cyberbullying.

DON'T SEND IT.
It's unsafe to send private info. If the wrong person got that info, they could use it to cyberbully you or someone else.

Take a Break

Technology makes it easy to "speak" without thinking. You can fire off an e-mail or post a comment any time. Just press "send" or "post," and your words are out there for others to read. But if you're feeling very angry or upset, stop before you press that button!

Everybody's done it. You've gotten so upset that you screamed something you didn't really mean. Then once you cooled down, you realized your mistake. Well, posting, texting, or e-mailing in anger is just the same. Instead, step away from the computer or set down the phone. Do something else that will calm you down. Read a book. Ride your bike. Walk your dog. Talk it over with your parents or other trusted adults too. They may have some ideas about how to respond that you didn't think of.

You thought you wrote a funny e-mail to your friend, but the reply you received seems really angry. In fact, your friend is attacking you for what you said. Now you're pretty upset.

What do you do?

Taking Control

If you're being cyberbullied, you may feel powerless. It's true you can't control someone else's choices. But you're definitely not powerless. You can take control of any cyberbullying situation by controlling your own response.

The best action is to get help. You don't have to deal with cyberbullying alone. Talk to a counselor, parent, or other trusted adult. They will help you deal with the situation. Report cyberbullying to ISPs and website monitors too. They're in the business of making sure cyberbullying has no place on their sites.

Protective Passwords

Make sure cyberbullies can't hack into your accounts. Create a hard-to-crack password using these tips.

Don't use your birthday.

Do include misspelled words.

Besides reporting cyberbullies, you can control how you respond. When you receive hurtful e-mails and text messages, the choice is yours. Sure, you could read them and write back. But those options are likely to make the cyberbullying continue and make you feel worse. Instead, delete messages from the bully without reading them. Then block messages from the cyberbully's account. Ignore the posts on social networking sites, and quit checking for new posts. Cyberbullies don't deserve your attention.

Do change passwords often.

Don't use the same password for every account.

Do include capital letters and numbers in unusual ways.

Don't use words that are easy to guess, such as your own name or a pet's name.

Bold Bystanders

When you see cyberbullying that doesn't involve you, walking away is an easy out. But ignoring it isn't a solution. Victims of cyberbullying are hoping you'll help. If you don't, you're just adding to the hurt.

There are some simple steps you can take to stop cyberbullying. One simple step is to refuse to pass along mean messages. If you read posts bashing someone else, don't just leave. Add positive posts to the discussion. Without arguing or attacking the bully, stand up to him or her. Politely point out that cruel comments are not welcome or wanted.

We Hate Jenny Club
Today at 8:23pm

Jenny is so stuck up! Click "like" and join the We Hate Jenny Club.

Like - Comment   👍11 💬6

Cassie Thompson
Today at 8:47pm

I like Jenny. She's always been nice to me. Your post is really mean.

Like - Comment   👍27 💬3

Kyle Becker
Today at 8:49pm

Jenny is my friend too. This page is mean! Take it down.

Like - Comment   👍15 💬1

Talk about it

You're online, and you come across a post by a kid at school. Her post says, "All the messages I get say I'm ugly and fat. Maybe they're right, and I am too ugly."

What do you do?

Tell a trusted adult about the bullying too. A victim may be too scared to talk about it. He or she needs you to do it. And if the victim asks you not to tell, do it anyway. Telling an adult is the right thing to do to get help and stop the cyberbully.

Sabrina Mastrangelo is Miss New York Teen USA 2012. But that didn't keep cyberbullying out of her life. When she checked a friend's social networking page, she found a shocking message. An anonymous poster wanted her friend dead. Sabrina couldn't imagine why her friend was targeted. "He's one of the nicest kids I've ever met in my life," she says. Sabrina took action by starting Teens United Long Island, a Facebook page. The page's goal is to bring teens together to raise awareness about cyberbullying and kick it out of cyberspace for good.

Sorry Cyberbullies

Think you've been a cyberbully in the past? That doesn't make you a bad person. It also doesn't mean you have to be a cyberbully in the future. The time to stop hurting others is now. But how?

When you want to break your cyberbullying habit, it helps to have a plan. Start by focusing on making a change. Instead of responding angrily to posts that upset you, take breaks so you can calm your emotions. Rather than continuing to slam others online, consider apologizing. Talk to trusted adults about your cyberbullying too. They can help you figure out why you're doing it. They can also help you find better ways to handle your problems.

I'M SORRY.

I really want to say some mean things right now. But I know there's a better way to handle this.

TALK about it

You hear that people at school have been spreading rumors about you. You'd like to text them a message that says to stop it or else. But you know that won't help.

What do you do?

Preventive Measures

You can't control what other people do. But you can take steps to protect yourself and make sure you aren't a cyberbully. Here are some ideas to keep in mind when using your cell phone, computer, or any other technology.

Don't share passwords with friends.

If you have an argument, your password could get passed around and your account could be hacked.

Give your passwords to your parents or guardians.

It may feel awkward to share messages from friends. But if you do, you'll have trusted adults on your side in case a cyberbully strikes.

Don't forward messages from other people without their permission.

The sender may consider the information private.

Wait before responding if you're angry or upset.

You'll be able to think and react more calmly if you take time away.

Think twice about the information you decide to share.

E-mails and texts are never guaranteed to stay private. Anything posted on the Internet could be there forever.

When cyberbullies use words and technology to hurt others, they can seem pretty powerful. But they're not. They're just meanies hiding behind a screen. When you take steps to stop cyberbullying, you're the one in control. You have the power to keep your online life safe and fun.

anonymous (uh-NON-uh-muhss)—written, done, or given by a person whose name is not known or made public

consequence (KAHN-suh-kwens)—the result of an action

hack (HAK)—to break into a computer system illegally

pose (POHZ)—to pretend to be someone else in order to trick others

revenge (ri-VENJ)—action taken in return for an injury or offense

rumor (ROO-mur)—something said by many people although it may not be true

stalk (STAWK)—to track a person in a secret way

suicide (SOO-uh-side)—the taking of one's own life

Read More

Nelson, Drew. *Dealing with Cyberbullies.*
Cyberspace Survival Guide. New York:
Gareth Stevens Pub., 2013.

Peterson, Judy Monroe. *How to Beat Cyberbullying.*
Beating Bullying. New York: Rosen Central, 2013.

Schwartz, Heather E. *Safe Social Networking.*
Tech Safety Smarts. Mankato, Minn.: Capstone
Press, 2013.

Internet Sites

FactHound offers a safe, fun way to find
Internet sites related to this book. All of the
sites on FactHound have been researched
by our staff.

Here's all you do:

Visit *www.facthound.com*

Type in this code: 9781429699440

Index